Us and The Creek

Illustrated by
Mr. Or's Scholars at
Mitchell Elementary School
Charleston, SC

Text by Merrie Koester, Ph.D.

Story text by Dr. Merrie Koester,
Director, Kids Teaching Flood Resilience
University of SC Center for Science Education

With grateful acknowledgement to
College of Charleston student assistant, Luna Riley

In Celebration of the Friends of Gadsden Creek!

We SEE YOU, across the street.

You are THERE for US.

We are HERE for YOU, too!

You used to be a big,
wide open marsh.
Full of fish and shrimps
for us to eat.

fish

shrimp

And with cool, beautiful water for swimming and Church baptisms.

Without your grasses and pluff mud, you can't hold onto the flood waters like you used to.

Now, there's not much of you left at ALL!

But we see you, trying to come back.
You're pushing right up through the street!

You are STRONG,
just like US!

You are still home
to so many
beautiful animals!

Your grasses and muds capture road pollution that would end up in our river!

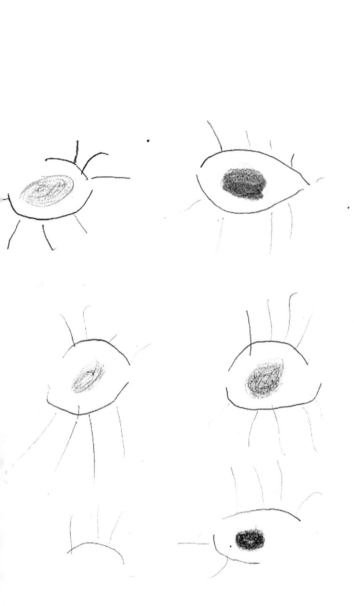

No one seems to notice you.
BUT WE DO!

When we are
in school
with Mr. Or,
there is joy.
There is care.

Can you hear us talking
about YOU?

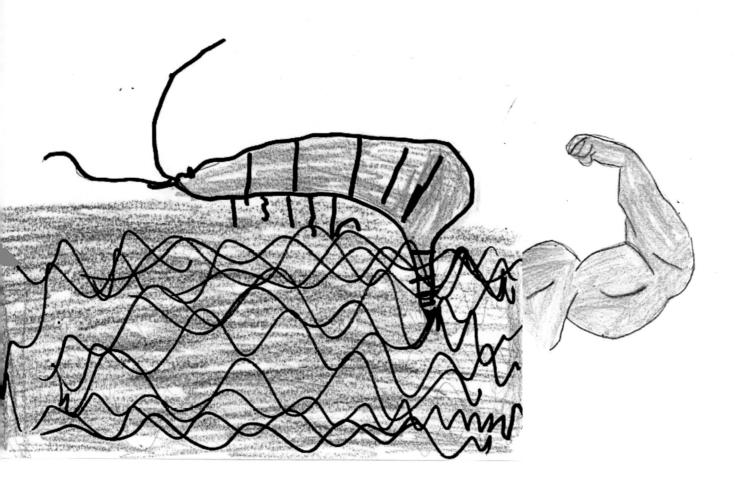

We know why you matter.
And why our community
matters, too!

This book is a celebration of the power of

OUR YOUTH to bring about

POSITIVE CHANGE

in our world.

This Science Artivism project emerged from the

Kids Teaching Flood Resilience initiative,

founded by Dr. Merrie Koester, University of South

Carolina Center for Science Education.

Gadsden Creek is your creek, too!

Drawing to Know About Animals and Plants
My Nature Journal

You can be a naturalist artist, too, just like Mr. Or's students. Use these blank pages to make drawings of your animal and plant friends and their homes! Include some facts you've learned about them, too.

Made in the USA
Monee, IL
28 October 2021